# Attrac
# & Feeding
# ORIOLES

**Stan Tekiela**

Adventure Publications
Cambridge, Minnesota

## Dedication

To my beautiful daughter Abby.

## Acknowledgments

Thanks to the Bird Collection, Bell Museum of Natural History, University of Minnesota (St. Paul) and the All Seasons Wild Bird Stores in Minnesota, which have been instrumental in obtaining some of the images in this book.

Thanks also to Jim and Carol Zipp, good friends and wild bird store owners, for reviewing this book.

## Credits

Front and back over photos of birds by Stan Tekiela except Bullock's Oriole by Rick and Nora Bowers. Front cover pattern by EVAsr/Shutterstock. Front cover bird icon by Roaddesign/Shutterstock.

All photos by Stan Tekiela except pg. 10 (Bullock's); pg. 11 (Scott's) by Rick and Nora Bowers, pg. 12 (Spot-breasted) by Luis Marquez/Shutterstock and pg. 13 (Audubon's) by Brian E. Small. All bird images are Baltimore Orioles unless otherwise labeled.

Edited by Sandy Livoti

Cover and book design by Jonathan Norberg

10 9 8 7 6 5 4 3 2 1

**Attracting & Feeding Orioles**

First Edition 2015, Second Edition 2022
Copyright © 2015 and 2022 by Stan Tekiela
Published by Adventure Publications
An imprint of AdventureKEEN
310 Garfield Street South
Cambridge, Minnesota 55008
(800) 678-7006
www.adventurepublications.net
All rights reserved
Printed in China
ISBN 978-1-64755-337-1 (pbk.); ISBN 978-1-64755-338-8 (ebook)

# TABLE OF CONTENTS

# All About Orioles

Of all of our backyard birds, just one seems to be a universal favorite—the Baltimore Oriole. The male's inky black feathers contrasting with the vibrant, flaming orange plumage make it an amazing sight at backyard feeders. The delicate yellow and orange colors of the female are great complements to the male.

Baltimore Orioles are well known for their remarkable series of clear whistle songs. You can hear them start to sing during the first few days of spring.

The Baltimore Oriole (*Icterus galbula*) is in the Icteridae family with 22 other species. Sometimes called Icterids, these birds are more commonly known as members of the Blackbird family, which is a huge group of birds.

Nine oriole species are found in the United States, including three in Canada. The Orchard Oriole is the same size as the Baltimore, but the male has a dark chestnut color. The Bullock's Oriole is the Baltimore's western counterpart in appearance, and the Scott's Oriole has a significant presence in parts of the West. The Hooded, Spot-breasted, Streak-backed, Altamira and Audubon's Orioles are much less common than the other species of orioles in the United States.

New World orioles occur only in North, Central and South America. They feed on insects and supplement their diet with nectar from flowers.

male

female

# FACTS

**Relative Size:** the Baltimore Oriole is smaller than an American Robin

**Length:** 7–8" (18–20 cm)

**Wingspan:** 10–11.5" (25–29 cm)

**Weight:** 1.2 oz. (34 g)

**Male:** black "hood" extending down the back, a rich, warm orange chest and belly, black wings with white and orange wing bars, thin and pointed gray bill

**Female:** similar to male but highly variable, with a varying black "hood" (the older the female, the darker and more complete the "hood"), yellow and dull orange chest and belly, gray-brown wings, white wing bars

**Juvenile:** similar to female except a gray belly and lighter colored wings with white wing bars

**Nest:** pendulous; 4–5" (10–13 cm) in diameter, 5–8" (13–20 cm) long; female and male weave strips of plant materials together and line the interior with fine grasses, plant down and animal hair

**Migration:** complete migrator; has a consistent, seasonal migration

**Food:** insects, fruit, nectar, sugar water solution

# RANGE & HABITAT

The Baltimore Oriole has one of the largest ranges of all the oriole species. It lives in open woodlands, preferring widely spaced, tall deciduous trees for nesting. It has adapted very well to human activities and readily nests in urban parks and backyards alike.

The other eight oriole species seen in the United States and Canada are shown on pages 10–13. The range of the Orchard Oriole is slightly more widespread than that of the Baltimore, but the Orchard is not nearly as common and the population is much less dense. They prefer wide-open habitats with scattered tall trees and are sometimes seen with Baltimore Orioles at feeders.

The Bullock's Oriole, a western cousin of the Baltimore, nests and feeds in open woodlands and also in riparian areas, which feature rivers and other watercourses.

Except for the Scott's and Hooded Orioles, all the other orioles have very limited ranges. Some barely reach into the United States and are not seen with any regularity.

Maps represent all oriole species in the United States and Canada.

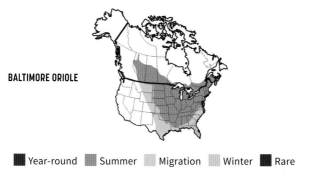

**BALTIMORE ORIOLE**

■ Year-round ■ Summer ■ Migration ■ Winter ■ Rare

**ORCHARD ORIOLE**

**BULLOCK'S ORIOLE**

Year-round  Summer  Migration  Winter  Rare

SCOTT'S ORIOLE

HOODED ORIOLE

Year-round   Summer   Migration   Winter   Rare

**SPOT-BREASTED ORIOLE**

**STREAK-BACKED ORIOLE**

■ Year-round ■ Summer ■ Migration ■ Winter ■ Rare

**ALTAMIRA ORIOLE**

**AUDUBON'S ORIOLE**

Year-round  Summer  Migration  Winter  Rare

# SONGS & CALLS

All of our oriole species are magnificent songsters. The rich, clear, whistle-like songs of male Baltimore Orioles piercing the forest canopy are sure signs of spring. Males sing loud advertisement songs from the treetops the very moment they arrive at their breeding territory from their wintering grounds in tropical regions. They sing to attract a mate and defend their territory from other males.

Female Baltimore Orioles also sing, which is fairly unusual for female songbirds of North America. Their songs are similar to those of the males, and they bolster the male songs. Sometimes pairs will even sing duets.

Male and female Baltimores give equally loud chattering or scolding calls. They make these calls when other bird species or predators approach or during aggressive encounters with other orioles. Whenever other birds hear an oriole's scolding call, they often join in to help drive away the threat.

### Quick-Tips

- Male Baltimore Orioles sing a series of strong whistle notes 2–8 times, with each phrase lasting 2–3 seconds
- Female Baltimore Orioles sing shorter and less complex songs than the males
- Male Orchard Oriole songs are loud, melodic phrases of 3–4 seconds alternating with chattering calls
- Unlike the advertisement songs of the breeding season, all orioles give chattering, scolding calls year-round

Orchard Oriole males sing a similar clear whistle song but with singsong phrasing interspersed with harsh chattering calls. Interestingly, the males sing mainly to attract a mate and not so much to defend a territory.

When you hear an oriole singing in spring, it is worth taking a few minutes to see if you can spot the bird. You just may see a male hopping around the branches, searching for an insect egg, a juicy beetle or other bug while he is singing. An appealing morsel of food will often interrupt a male that has begun a song phrase. After snapping up the tidbit, he continues to sing again.

All oriole species are extremely vocal while they are establishing territories and attracting a mate. Males do not sing as much during nest construction, after the eggs are laid or during incubation. They will, however, continue to give scolding calls.

During the nest construction stage, females keep their singing to a minimum. They don't want to draw any attention to themselves while working at the nest site. Later, they don't want to attract unwanted interest to their nests, which are holding eggs or babies.

male

female

# NESTS

Orioles make unique large nests. Unlike the familiar open cup nests, orioles painstakingly weave hanging sock-like nests. These are called pendulous nests because they hang and swing like a pendulum.

Females typically return to the same area to nest, often to a tree near her nesting site of the previous year or close to where she hatched. Only one-year-old females and older will nest.

The female does the majority of the construction. It takes her about 6–8 days to build a nest, depending on the availability of nesting material and the cooperation of the weather. It can take upwards of two weeks to complete a nest during periods of wet, windy weather. Males will occasionally bring in some nesting material, but the lion's share comes from the female.

Oriole nests are meticulously woven together with thin strips of plant material, such as grapevine bark and milkweed stems. Occasionally the female will rob fibers from an old nest to make the new one. Nests are almost always gray, but people who cut strands of colored yarn and offer them to orioles in old suet feeders may see their yarn carefully woven in the nests.

It's not common, but sometimes a female will reclaim an old nest and refurbish it to use a second time. Many times these nests are so well constructed that they last for two or more years without being repaired.

The female looks for a nesting site high in a tree near the ends or tips of a hanging branch. She selects a spot with forking branches that have a number of leaves around them to help conceal the nest. Most nests are constructed 30 feet up or higher. This helps reduce the chances that predators, such as squirrels and raccoons, will raid the nest.

When the female begins construction, she first loops some long hanging fibers. She doesn't tie any actual knots, but all the poking will weave the natural material in and out to make the basic sock-shaped frame. She painstakingly weaves each added strip of plant material into the structure with her long, sharp, needle-like bill. After all, her treetop nest needs to be extremely strong to withstand the high winds and driving rain of spring.

The nest entrance is at the top. The pendulous shape is slender at the top, with a wider, rounded bottom to accommodate the eggs, the mother and eventually the chicks. The female finishes construction by lining the interior cup with fine, soft plant materials.

# EGGS, CHICKS & JUVENILES

Baltimore Orioles nest only once per season, but new evidence shows that some have two broods per year. Chicks hatch naked and helpless and cannot regulate their own body temperature. The mother must continue to sit on them (brood) until they have enough feathers to keep warm. She leaves only to eat and defecate.

Within just 12–14 days of hatching, the baby orioles are starting to climb up and out of the nest (fledge). By this time they are juveniles, full size and look like the female. The youngsters hop around on the branches of the birth tree, waiting for their parents to come and feed them. Within a few more weeks, they are following the parents around and fluttering their wings to beg for food. While following their parents, juveniles find the feeding stations that are offering some of their favorite foods, such as grape jelly and orange halves.

**Broods:** 1 per season

**Clutch Size:** 3–7 eggs (4–5 average)

**Egg Length:** 8–1" (2–2.5 cm)

**Egg Color:** pale gray to light blue and marked with brown and black blotches

**Incubation:** 12–14 days; female incubates

**Hatchlings:** naked except for sparse tufts of down feathers, with eyes and ears sealed shut

**Fledging:** 12–14 days

# ORIOLE TRIVIA

- The Baltimore Oriole is named after Lord Baltimore, whose family crest is bright orange.

- The Baltimore's scientific name *Icterus galbula* is Latin and means "a small yellow bird."

- The name "Oriole" originates from the Latin *aureus*, meaning "golden" and describes the Eurasian Golden Oriole, an Old World species that is not related to our North American orioles.

- Henry David Thoreau called orioles "golden robins."

- Baltimore and Bullock's Orioles were once grouped together as one species, called the Northern Oriole. Now they are recognized as separate species.

- Only Baltimore and Orchard Orioles are found in the eastern United States and eastern Canada. Except for Spot-breasted Orioles, the rest are western species.

- Even though male orioles are brightly colored and conspicuous, they are often heard singing from the treetops long before they are seen.

- Individual males have unique phrasing and cadence, making it possible to identify specific males.

- By the end of summer, the males are usually singing an abbreviated version of their breeding song.

- Female orioles also sing. This is a rather uncommon characteristic for North American songbird females.

- The average life span of a Baltimore is 5–10 years. Some individuals have lived as long as 11 years.

- As female orioles age, they develop a darker "hood," making some appear like adult males.

- First-year males have brown on their heads and look similar to the adult females.

- Orioles have excellent memories. In spring they often return to the same feeding stations to feed from the same reliable food sources from the previous year.

- Orioles are the foremost consumers of a variety of harmful caterpillars that damage trees. They feed mostly on insects during summer, and caterpillars are the main item on the menu.

- Orioles use their long, narrow pointed bills to probe into flowers, curled leaves and other tight places in search of insects, insect eggs, caterpillars and larvae.

Hooded Oriole

- The autumn diet is fresh and dried fruit and nectar.

- Male orioles arrive on the breeding grounds more than a week ahead of females in spring. Rarely do males show up before leaves start to grow on trees.

- Older males return to their breeding territory of choice from the previous year.

- Males are friendly to each other before the females arrive. Once the ladies appear, male orioles start fighting to establish territories and claim mates.

- Mature American Elms were the favorite of nesting orioles before Dutch elm disease killed so many trees.

- With only one brood per season, orioles are unlike most other birds, which try to raise two or sometimes three broods each season.

- Brown-headed Cowbirds lay their mottled white eggs in the unattended nests of other birds. Orioles tend to reject unfamiliar eggs such as these.

- Orioles are true migrators, flying away each fall to the tropics of Mexico and Central and South America.

- Females and juveniles begin to migrate in August, several weeks before the males.

- During winter in the tropics, orioles frequent shady coffee plantations and banana and cacao farms.

- Orioles migrate during the night, using the stars to help navigate. It may take them a month to get from southern Texas back to the northern states and into Canada in spring.

- In recent years more orioles are overwintering in such places as southern Florida and southern Texas, as well as along the Gulf Coast states.

Orchard Oriole

# Feeding Orioles

Feeding orioles is the best way to see these marvelous birds frequently. Normally they eat insects high up in the canopy of trees, but with just a few sweet offerings you can draw them down to your feeders.

You can tempt orioles with four items. Perhaps the most common way to attract them is with orange halves. Another surefire way to get orioles to visit is to put out feeders with sugar water solution. Grape jelly is the best treat to bring in orioles, and setting out dishes with mealworms rounds out the diet.

One of the easiest ways to attract orioles is to cut some fresh oranges in half and offer them sunny-side up at your feeding station. Halved oranges allow orioles easy access to the soft, juicy flesh of the fruit.

Just drive a nail or small screw into a wooden platform feeder, deck railing or even a tree trunk and impale the orange half. You may need to make a small cut in the rind to help get the nail through. You will find that other  birds, such as House Finches, also eat orange halves and will help clean them out down to the skin.

Offer a sugar water solution similar to the homemade nectar you give to your hummingbirds. Make a solution using white sugar and water. To mix a solution, use white sugar and water. Don't use brown sugar, honey or imitation sweeteners. These products won't work, and in some cases they can harm birds. Do not add food coloring.

Most flowers produce a 20 percent sugar (sucrose) solution. To match this, mix four parts water to one part white granulated sugar. This will make a 25 percent sugar solution. Some recommend a six to one solution. It's a good idea to boil the mixture for a few minutes; this will help to keep it from spoiling before the orioles finish it. Allow the solution to cool before filling your feeders. Hot solution can burn you badly when it spills. It can also crack glass or melt plastic containers.

If your orioles are going through the nectar solution very quickly and you are replacing it daily or every other day, you can skip the boiling method. Just dissolve the sugar in warm tap water and pour it into the container. If your solution is disappearing slowly, commercial items are available to help extend the life of the solution.

The most successful way to attract orioles to feeding stations is to set out grape jelly. The kind that orioles prefer tends to be the cheapest generic brand you can find and is probably due to the added sugar.

Other birds, such as Gray Catbirds, House Finches and Red-bellied Woodpeckers, also love grape jelly. Be prepared to purchase a number of large jars because the jelly will be eaten quickly. Don't be surprised if the birds stop coming to your orange halves once you have started putting out grape jelly.

Some people simply fill cleaned-out orange halves with grape jelly. This is an easy and much less messy way to offer jelly. Orioles will come to other flavors of jelly, but I have found that grape is their favorite.

Offering mealworms in a shallow tray is another great way to attract orioles. Since orioles are mainly insect eaters, they will eagerly gobble up mealworms. You can offer both live and also dried mealworms. When the spring season  is cold and there is not much insect activity, offering mealworms is the ideal way for orioles to get their much-needed protein.

Mealworms are the larval stage of a type of grain beetle (*Tenebrio molitor*). They are sold in plastic containers and should be kept in the refrigerator, where they can remain fresh for 1–2 months. A single oriole can eat dozens of mealworms each day, so purchasing them in the hundreds or thousands is often recommended.

When times are tough and the spring weather is not cooperating, the returning orioles are desperate for any kind of protein. When this happens, suet, usually set out for woodpeckers, is an alternative food they will eat.

They will visit suet feeders and take the fatty offerings, often discarding the seeds and other bits of food they don't like. Some suet cakes are infused with insects. These can be good to offer orioles early in spring.

Fresh fruit also provides other nutrition to orioles during spring, so put out a shallow plate of cut fruit. Good choices include oranges, grapefruit, apples, raisins, cherries, bananas and peaches. Other birds will also find these foods to their liking and will be attracted to your feeders as a bonus.

# FEEDING Q&A

### Preserves vs. jelly—what's the difference?

Fruit preserves have chunks of real fruit; jelly does not. While orioles will eat preserves, they prefer smooth jelly. They will come to a variety of flavors, but they have a strong preference for grape. Although strawberry, peach and other jellies provide the level of sugar desired by orioles, grape jelly always seems to win out.

### If a small cup of grape jelly is good, is a large bowl better?

Offering grape jelly in small containers helps the orioles reach and retrieve the food without physically getting into the container. A large bowl of jelly will only invite the birds to climb inside, risking the chances of coating their clean feathers with the gooey treat. The result would be disastrous for the birds, so keep your jelly containers small, approximately 2–3 inches in diameter and only 1–2 inches deep.

## When should I put out my oriole feeders in spring?

Orioles will suddenly show up one morning in spring. They migrate at night, so usually the first time you will notice them is the morning they arrive. The males arrive first and start to sing from the tops of trees. Depending on where you are in the country, this can be anywhere from the first of April in the South to the first of May in northern states and Canada. The exact dates are often different from year to year, depending on local weather patterns. So it's always good to have your feeders up on time and waiting for their arrival.

## When is it too late to put up oriole feeders?

You can put up oriole feeders at any time during the breeding season. Even when you don't see any orioles in the area, chances are they are there, high up in the trees. Putting up a feeder even in the middle of summer can still attract orioles.

## My orioles stopped coming to my feeders. Did I do something wrong?

In early spring the orioles mob feeders, scarfing up jar after jar of grape jelly and bags of oranges. Even after the females arrive and nesting starts, the parents spend a lot of time visiting feeders. Then suddenly one day they stop showing up. This is usually associated with the hatching of the young. The adult orioles need to concentrate on bringing home protein-rich insects for their growing chicks, and that is usually the time when most people notice the orioles have stopped coming to their feeders. Just be patient and wait a couple weeks. Suddenly the adults will start to show up again—but this time they will have their hungry chicks with them.

## What if my nectar feeders go dry when I'm on vacation?

Orioles feed mainly on insects and don't depend on our feeders. They use our feeders as a supplement to their regular diet. If you go out of town and your grape jelly or orange halves get eaten, the orioles will simply obtain their nutritional requirements from wild sources or other nearby feeders. They have wings, and they know how to use them to find other food sources. When you return home, refill your feeders with grape jelly and fresh orange halves and they will come back none the worse for wear.

## If I have more than one oriole coming to my feeders, should I put out more feeders?

Yes, it's always a good idea to put out more feeders. It is best to offer a variety of feeding stations or places for the birds to feed. If you have many individuals coming to your feeders, it allows them to feed without having to wait or fight with other birds for the food. So put up orange halves at one feeding station and grape jelly at another. Your sugar water feeders should be set up at a third location.

## What about ants and bees?

Anytime you put out sugar water, grape jelly or orange halves, you will attract ants and bees. Ants are easy to deter if you have your feeders on poles or other feeding stations. There are many products on the market that will repel ants. Simply smear these products on poles, and the ants will stop coming.

Bees are a bit trickier since they fly to feeders. Use bee guards on your sugar water feeders to help reduce the number of visiting bees.

## Should I stop feeding orioles at the end of summer?

Feeding orioles all summer long is one of the many highlights of summertime backyard bird feeding. Their bright plumages and cheerful songs are just a couple of the reasons why we feed them. Your sweet offerings won't stop them from migrating, so there is no need to stop feeding them. Depending on where you live, one morning in late August or early September you will wake up and the orioles will be gone. The good news is you can look forward to their return the following spring.

# Oriole Feeders

Just about any kind of feeder will work for orioles. As long as the grape jelly, orange half, mealworms or sugar water solution can be seen, the birds will find the feeder. Homemade wooden feeders are great family projects and make wonderful gifts for homeowners. Consider decorating part of a wooden feeder with orange paint or adding an orange ribbon to help the birds find the food.

Many oriole feeders are orange, but red feeders and wooden feeders also attract orioles very well. Simply add an orange half to natural-colored feeders, and the birds will soon come for the sweet treat.

Oriole feeders may have one or more small, shallow cups to fill with grape jelly and also a metal peg for impaling an orange half. Hang these feeders to draw in any and all orioles in the neighborhood.

If orioles are spilling the nectar in your hummingbird feeder, try a nectar feeder made especially for orioles.

## Quick-Tips

- Oriole feeders do not need to be completely orange
- Drive a nail or screw into your wooden platform feeder and twist on an orange half to attract orioles to it
- Orioles prefer the most sugary, inexpensive grape jelly over all flavors of the more pricey varieties
- Use a four to one or six to one sugar water solution to feed to your orioles

# FEEDER TYPES

**Grape Jelly Feeder:** Some of the best jelly feeders are large plastic or wooden feeders with a couple holes to hold small plastic cups. These are often covered with a roof of some sort to keep out rain. They are usually orange and can hang from a hook at a feeding station or may be mounted on top of a pole. However, just about any small container will work to hold grape jelly. You can reuse a small margarine tub, for example, and screw it to a scrap of wood. A plastic container that can hold just two or three large spoonfuls of grape jelly is all that is needed.

**Sugar Water Feeder:** These oriole feeders are often flat plate-like structures with a number of openings where the birds can insert their beaks and get the sugar water. They are typically orange and look very similar to hummingbird feeders. Often they have a central metal pin or stalk from which the feeder hangs. Sugar water feeders frequently have built-in ant moats that you fill with water or vegetable oil to stop ants from getting to the nectar. They come apart easily, which makes for trouble-free cleaning.

**Orange Half Feeder:** Constructed of wood and often looks like a tiny house with a miniature roof. All styles have a nail or screw for impaling an appealing orange half. A large landing pad or place for orioles to stand while feeding on the fruit is critical.

**Mealworm Feeder:** Sometimes just a small plastic butter tub works well to offer orioles mealworms. A shallow dish or a water dish from a flowerpot can also double as a good mealworm feeder.

Many types of mealworm feeders have "gates" to keep out some larger birds while allowing orioles and other smaller birds to enter. These effectively stop some birds from flying in and scarfing down all the mealworms in one visit.

**Window Feeder:** Typically made of clear plastic and usually a small feeder trimmed in bright red or orange. Suction cups hold this lightweight apparatus tightly to window surfaces. These feeders are great for attracting orioles to see up close. They don't hold a lot of nectar and need to be refilled often, but they are easy to open and clean.

# PLACING FEEDERS

Feeding orioles is a wonderful way to enhance your backyard feeding stations. Placement of oriole feeders is very similar to the placement of your seed feeders.

You can add orange halves to your current feeders just about anywhere they will fit. Just pound a nail into a wooden feeder and gently twist on an orange half. You can also wedge an orange half in the fork of a tree branch if you don't have a lot of squirrels. These critters will dislodge the orange and take it away to eat.

All feeding stations should be placed in clear view of your house. After all, we feed birds to see and admire the many colorful species coming and going and to enjoy the lively activity. So the best feeding stations are those that include different kinds of feeders.

Feeding stations need to be in places that will help deter pesky squirrels, raucous raccoons and bears. To keep squirrels away from the food, attach a standard squirrel baffle to each feeder pole, following the basic placement rules of 5 and 8 feet. That means feeders should be at least 5 feet off the ground and at least 8 feet from any other surface from which a squirrel can jump. This includes trees, houses, sheds, charcoal or gas grills, birdbaths, patio furniture and anything else a squirrel can climb to jump onto the feeders.

Raccoons are skillful climbers and can do much more damage to feeding stations than lightweight squirrels. Large raccoon-style baffles will keep them and also squirrels off the feeders. These should be installed using the same guides as the squirrel baffles.

Baffles are metal tubes that prevent hungry animals from climbing your shepherd's hooks or feeder poles and accessing the bird food. They are simple devices and extremely worthwhile to purchase. If you are handy, you can fashion one from a stovepipe.

Bears, however, can get into and tear apart nearly any feeder regardless of a baffle, so take in your feeders at night if you live in bear country. This is the best and safest way to avert nighttime commotion and damage to your feeding stations.

When you place feeders, provide a variety to attract orioles. Put out a simple dish for grape jelly, a board with several nails to hold several orange halves, and a small dish of mealworms. Sugar water feeders are very important and will help attract more orioles. Remember to hang some window feeders to bring the birds closer for even more enjoyment.

# Maintaining Feeders & Good Practices

Feeder maintenance is essential for the overall health of orioles. How often you clean your feeders depends on the situation. For example, has the grape jelly offering become dirty or overly messy? Has sugar water spilled around the area? Are the mealworm dishes filling with water or dirt? Cleaning feeders is more important during the hot spells of summer than during springtime and late summer.

Anytime you see the sugar water solution become cloudy, it is time to clean your feeder and refill it with fresh solution. There are a number of products on the market that will extend the life of nectar by several days, even during the dog days of summer. Most of these are liquid preservatives, and all are safe for the birds.

A number of transmissible diseases are associated with birds, including orioles, and their droppings. To be safe, use good hygiene practices and take some basic precautions when filling or cleaning your feeders.

For instance, when you clean the feeders, wear rubber gloves. After cleaning, vigorously wash your gloved hands and cleaning brushes with warm, soapy water. Use paper towels to pat dry, and discard the towels.

# CLEANING YOUR FEEDERS

Always try to use rubber gloves when handling your feeders and cleaning the feeding area because there are several diseases that can be picked up from bird droppings. *Histoplasma capsulatum* is a fungus in soils that is deposited from bird and bat droppings. Many people who contract histoplasmosis don't develop symptoms, but some exhibit mild flu-like symptoms. Rarely, other people can suffer serious complications.

Cryptococcosis is another fungal disease found in the environment, and it also comes from bird droppings. Often associated with pigeon droppings, it is best to wear rubber gloves and a mask when cleaning up scat on feeders and around sites where large numbers of birds gather. Like histoplasmosis, many people don't suffer any symptoms. Some just come down with symptoms of a mild flu.

West Nile virus is carried by mosquitoes. Orioles and other birds contract it but don't transfer it to humans, so there is no need to be concerned about getting this disease from your feeders.

Keeping your feeding station clean and refreshing the site are quick and easy ways to stop the spread of avian disease and other diseases from bird droppings.

You should wet-clean your feeder if there are obvious signs of mold or mildew. Dead birds near feeders or on them are another indicator that a major wet cleaning is needed. Use a sanitizing solution of one part bleach to nine parts warm water, or purchase a commercial bird feeder cleaning solution.

Oftentimes all it takes is a simple rinse of the entire feeder between each refilling. Only when black mold starts to grow inside the nectar container should you spend extra time cleaning with soap, water and a brush. Dismantle the feeder as much as possible and scour with your scrub brushes and cleaning solution. Clean inside and out and rinse well with hot water. Allow the feeder to dry thoroughly overnight or lay the parts out in the sunlight before reassembling and refilling it. Then watch as the orioles come to partake again and enjoy.

# About the Author

Naturalist, wildlife photographer and writer Stan Tekiela is the originator of the popular Backyard Bird Feeding Guides series that includes *Attracting & Feeding Hummingbirds*. Stan has authored more than 190 educational books, including field guides, quick guides, nature books, children's books and more, presenting many species of animals and plants.

With a Bachelor of Science degree in natural history from the University of Minnesota and as an active professional naturalist for more than 30 years, Stan studies and photographs wildlife throughout the United States and Canada. He has received national and regional awards for his books and photographs and is also a well-known columnist and radio personality. His syndicated column appears in more than 25 newspapers, and his wildlife programs are broadcast on a number of Midwest radio stations. You can follow Stan on Facebook, Instagram and Twitter, or contact him via his website, naturesmart.com.